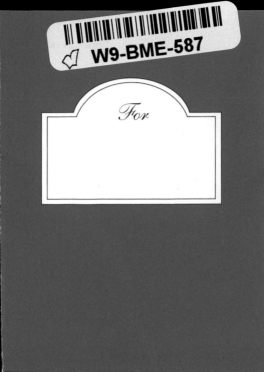

For

Home
Is Where
The Heart Is

By Beth Mende Conny

Illustrated by Dara Boland

Peter Pauper Press, Inc.

WHITE PLAINS, NEW YORK

For Aunt Dotty and Aunt Ethel, with love

Copyright © 1997
Peter Pauper Press, Inc.
202 Mamaroneck Avenue
White Plains, NY 10601
All rights reserved
ISBN 0-88088-820-2
Printed in China
7 6 5 4 3 2

Home
Is Where
The Heart Is

INTRODUCTION

Home is not just a place
but a state of mind, a sacred
space we carry with us in
heart and soul. Filled with
warmth, joy, and those
we love, it's a celebration
of life.

Let us celebrate together
then in the pages that follow
for, truly, as a wise little girl
named Dorothy once said,
there's no place like home.

B. M. C.

In the home, we learn
the most important of
four-letter words—love.

A house is built brick
by brick, a home heart
by heart.

The home is a welcome
rest area on the busy road
of life.

The home is the school
in which we first learn
life's lessons.

Home is the stage on
which we rehearse our roles
and develop our character.

A home is a place of
comfort, familiarity,
warmth, and joy.

*H*ome is a place to hang
your hat—and heart.

Home's the place where we
can kick off our shoes and
kick up our heels.

*H*ome is a place we
carry with us—
in memory and heart.

In the home, we learn
to treat others—and
ourselves—with respect.

*H*ome—where many
a battle is fought and
peace treaty signed.

*H*omes are
like snowflakes—
no two are alike.

*E*ven the smallest
homes have infinite
room for love.

The home is a jewelry box
that holds our most
precious belongings—
our loved ones.

The family is a world
unto itself, the home
the universe in which
it spins.

*T*o feel at home with our
family is to feel at home
with the world.

*F*amily—that miraculous
group of folks who note
our imperfections but
accept us just the same.

When all is right in the
family, all is right in
the world.

How nice that the
first thing to greet us when
we enter this world is
our family.

We begin and end in the
bosom of our families.

Time passes,
family remains.

Close families bridge
distances with love.

A family may not live
under one roof, still it
lives in one heart.

Close families may head in
different directions, yet they
travel the same road.

We *can* go home again, in heart, body, and mind.

Loving families keep the
porch lights burning.

When we return home,
we return to ourselves.

In our parents' home,
we become kids again.

*F*amily reunions reunite
us with ourselves.

The extended family
extends our love.

Family traditions are
the roots that keep us
grounded.

*H*oliday traditions give the
home a special glow.

In the home we celebrate
birthdays, anniversaries, life.

A family is not greater
than its parts, but greater
because of them.

*F*amily—the world's greatest team.

A family is a work
in progress.

A good family, like good
health, is invaluable.

Families, like true friends,
hold us to higher standards.

*H*umor is the lubricant
that keeps family
gears turning.

Families are the embers
that keep us warm in a
sometimes cold world.

*T*he family is the
seed from which all
growth begins.

*F*amily values—the filters
through which we
view the world.

The sights, smells,
and sounds of home are
the threads that weave the
fabric of our lives.

It is in the family that we
learn to share—meals,
space, laughter, tears.

Like a magnet,
the kitchen draws
family together.

*H*ome cooking fills
the tummy and
nourishes the soul.

Many modest homes
are filled with priceless
masterpieces—crayon
drawings on refrigerators.

A home is filled
with mementos that mark
the beginnings of great
times to come.

A living room is a learning room, where family gathers and life's lessons unfold.

Our homes are mirrors
that reflect our tastes
and values.

Home is an easy chair—
warm, comfortable, familiar.

Where there is room in
the heart, there is room
in the home.

A happy home is furnished
with love and laughter.

*J*ust as the sun filters
through a window and
brightens a room, love filters
through a family and
brightens the world.

No matter how far
from home we travel,
we always long for our
own beds.

Kitchens—where great
food and conversations
are served.

Family gives us a boost as
we reach for the stars.

*H*ome is a
state of mind.

When the going gets rough,
family smoothes the edges.

*T*rue love is *home*made.

Dorothy was right—
there truly is no place
like home.